This is a highly entertaining collection of mammals, birds, reptiles and insects, past and present, seen in some very comic and curious circumstances. They are presented alphabetically and in glorious full color. Children of all ages will have great fun identifying the animals in their strange situations.

A comic and curious collection of **animals, birds** and other **creatures**

By BOBBIE CRAIG

MODERN PUBLISHING
A Division of Unisystems, Inc.
New York, New York 10022
Printed in Belgium

Aa is for ant, alligator, armadillo, ape and adder asleep in the afternoon.

Bb *is for* bear, badger, buffalo, beaver, boa, bandicoot, baboon and bison at a birthday party.

Cc *is for* cat, camel, cow, crow, cobra and crocodile counting cards.

Dd *is for* dormouse, duck, dog, deer and donkey dancing daintily.

Ee *is for* elk, eland, elephant, emu and eagle enjoying Easter eggs.

Ff *is for* foal, falcon, fly, fox and fennec having fun at the fair.

Gg *is for* gorilla, goat, gerbil, giraffe and gull gathering grapes.

Hh *is for* hamsters, hippopotamus, horse, hedgehog, hyena and humming bird haymaking at harvest time.

16

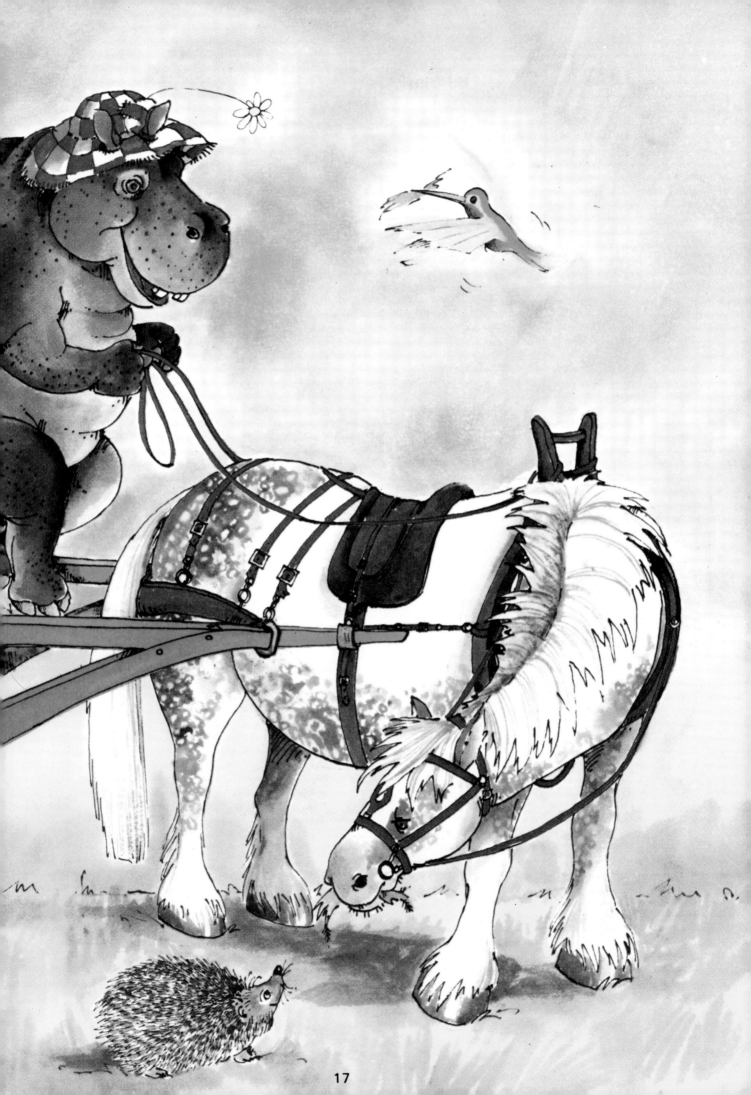

Ii *is for* iguana, impala, ibex and ibis ill with indigestion.

ibex

ibis

Jj *is for* jackdaw, jaguar, jellyfish and jackal jogging through the jungle.

Kk *is for* kestrel, kudu, koala, kinkajou and kangaroo flying kites.

L1 *is for* lion, llama, ladybug, lynx, lapwing, lizard and leopard lounging by the lake.

Mm *is for* monkey, mouse, mandrill, mongoose and mamba on a merry-go-round.

Nn *is for* nightingale, nightjar, newt and narwhal getting nervous at night.

Oo

is for ox, opossum, otter, octopus, orang-utan, okapi and ostrich in an orchestra.

Pp is for puma, panda, pelican, penguin, pigeon and pig painting pictures.

Qq *is for* quagga, quails and quetzal queuing to see the queen bee.

Rr *is for* rat, rattlesnake, razorbill, rhinoceros and rabbit running in a race.

Ss *is for* squirrel, seal, snail, stoat, skunk and scorpion sunbathing at the seaside.

Tt *is for* turkey, toucan, toad, tweeter, turtle and trout tobogganing in twos.

Uu *is for* urchin, umbrella bird and uakari under umbrellas.

V v *is for* vole, viper and vicuna looking at various vests.

SALE OF
VESTS
VARIOUS SIZES.

Ww *is for* wallaby, warthog, walrus, woodpecker, wolf, and weasels washing on a windy day.

Xx *as in* ox and fox examining x-rays.

46

Yy *is for* yaffingale, yak and yellowhammer yawning in their beds.

Zz *is for* zebras zigzagging at the zoo.

Tired tiger telling us that's the end

Laughing lion longing to learn to count

1 hippopotamus humming

2 dinosaurs dancing

3 hyenas hurrying

4 bears boxing

5 dragons drinking

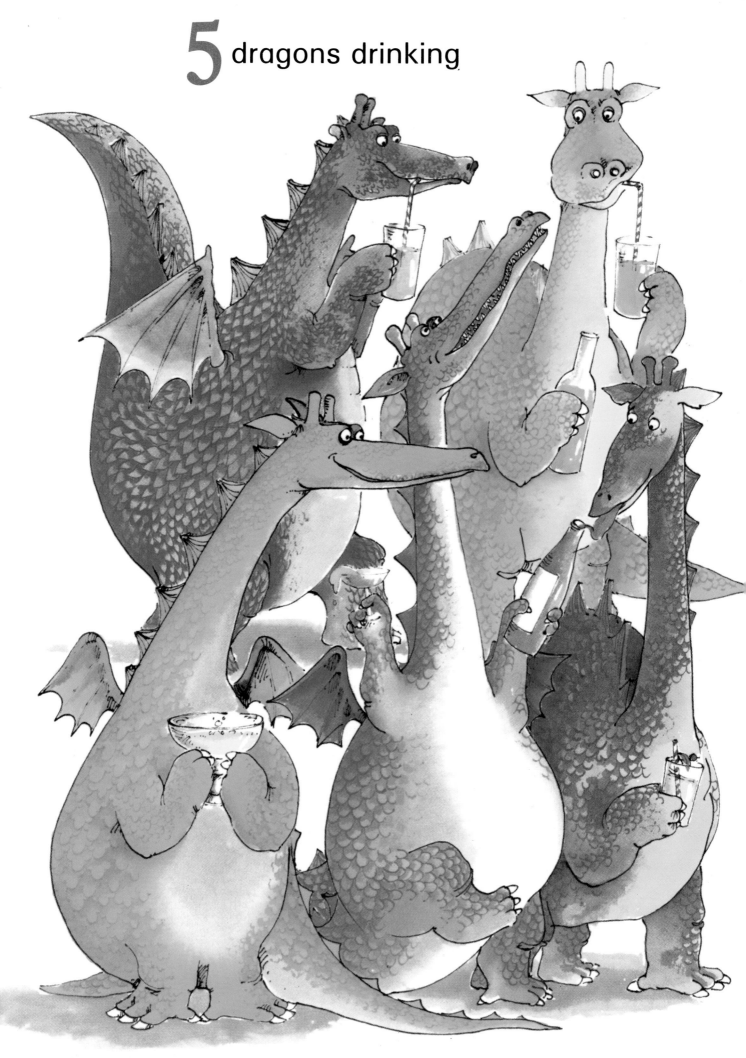

6 lizards leaping

7 snakes snoozing

8 penguins picnicking

9 monkeys making mischief

10 rabbits racing

The animal alphabet

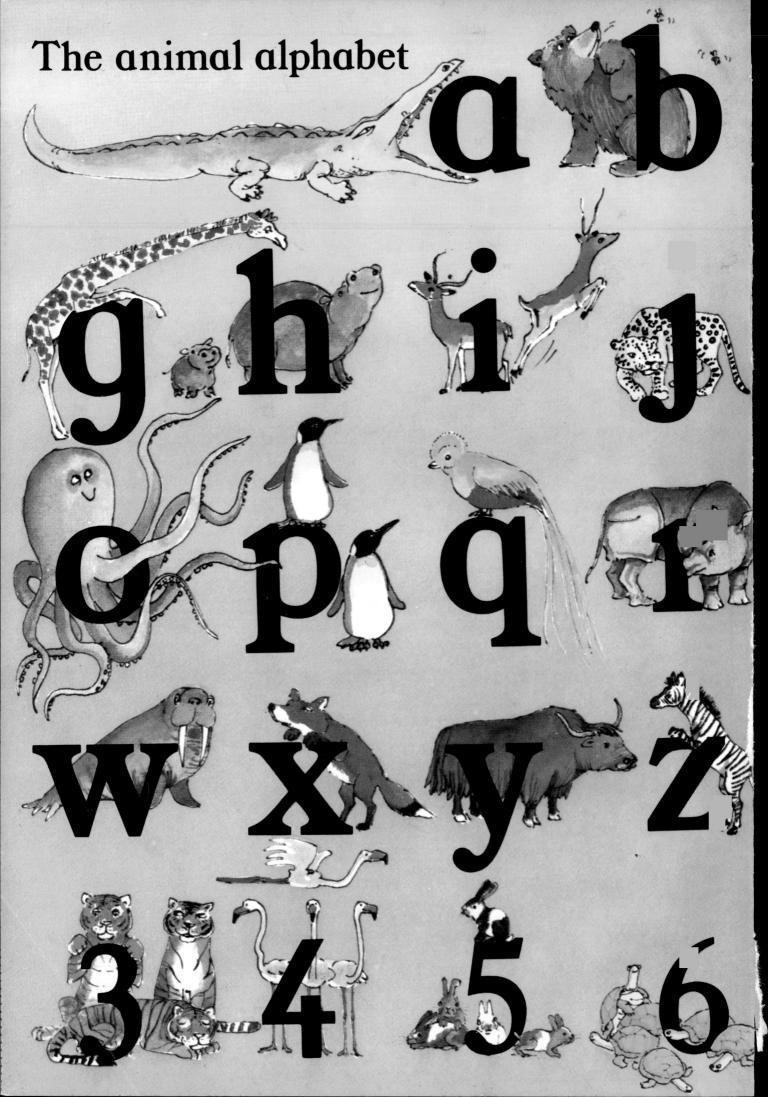